PLANE SPEAKING

PLANE SPEAKING

The Wit and Wisdom of Michael O'Leary

reverently compiled by Paul Kilduff

First published in Great Britain
2010 by Aurum Press Ltd
7 Greenland Street, London NW1 0ND
www.aurumpress.co.uk

A catalogue record for this book is available
from the British Library.

ISBN-13 978 1 84513 541 6

1 3 5 7 9 10 8 6 4 2
 2010 2012 2014 2013 2011

This book is printed on paper certified by the
Forest Stewardship Council as coming
from a forest that is well managed according to
strict environmental, social and economic
standards.

Design by Roger Hammond
Printed by MPG Books, Bodmin, Cornwall

Contents

Introduction 7

Passengers 9

Flying 14

Low Fares 17

In-flight 20

Baggage 26

Customer Service 29

'Peacocks' 33

Staff 36

Aircraft 39

History 42

Present Day 45

Investors 48

Corporate Life 52

'Eco-Nuts' 55

Security 62

Politicians 65

The European
Commission 69

'BA-stards' 74

easyJet 78

Other Airlines 81

Ireland 87

'Britain's Awful
Airports' 90

Airports 93

Destinations 97

Publicity 101

Love 107

Home 113

Sport 117

Wealth 121

Retirement 125

Introduction

MICHAEL O'LEARY has been described as 'a kind and gentle, caring and thoughtful, sensitive and saintly human being widely beloved by all Ryanair's 6,500 people and its 66 million passengers.' By his own communications chief.

O'Leary has transformed a tiny Irish airline operating one turbo-prop fifteen-seater aircraft on the Waterford to Gatwick route in 1985 into the largest airline in Europe, with 200 aircraft, 950 routes, 40 bases and 1,300 daily departures, all generating €2.4 billion in profits in the past 11 years. He has not achieved this by taking the conventional approach to airline management – or to PR. Then again, given Ryanair's stupendous success, perhaps suggesting that your own passengers 'fuck off' should become conventional management practice?

Here is a visionary who ended free in-flight food, charged for hold baggage, shut check-in desks, introduced compulsory online check-in and might yet make you stand on a flight or pay a pound to have a pee. He is happy to arrive for his press conferences dressed as Santa, Caesar, the Pope or St Patrick. He has a view about most things, whether you want to hear it or not. You may be sorry you asked, or indeed that you didn't even ask. Either way, it'll probably cost you money. Would you like to buy a scratchcard, by the way?

The Gospel According to O'Leary has now been compiled. It includes cheap phonecards, smokeless cigarettes, non-reclining seats, pitiless commercial sense, and lots of swearing. None of this occurred to orthodox philosophers like Plato, Kierkegaard and John Stuart Mill. But then, as the great man himself opines: 'I'm a genius, but I'm just too humble to say so.'

PASSENGERS

'We're not going to fall for any of this old management bullshit, or MBA rubbish about clichéd concerns for passengers.'

. . .

'Green protesters are our best passengers. They're always flying off to their demonstrations.'

. . .

On funeral-goers being Ryanair's most profitable passengers: 'They book late because they don't tend to have much notice, and they tend to be price-insensitive because they have to travel.'

. . .

'Our ideal passenger is someone with a pulse and a credit card, who will follow the simple instructions to lower our costs to the maximum.'

. . .

'A bunch of fucking do-gooders brought a case against Ryanair, claiming its identification policy discriminates against asylum seekers. What the fuck? These people are in England seeking asylum and now they want to fly around Europe? Well, they can't do it on Ryanair.'

. . .

PLANE SPEAKING

'The Disability Rights Commission wouldn't fucking know how much a wheelchair costs if it jumped up and bit them. We kept getting people who just didn't fancy the long walk to the plane and declared themselves to be in need of assistance. You don't expect to turn up at Bluewater shopping centre on the bus and expect the driver to wheel you round the shops.'

. . .

On allegations of flying lager louts on stag weekends: 'We call them the Chianti louts heading to villas in Tuscany and the South of France. If you think they're setting a bad example I would point you to lunatics like Robert Mugabe. He didn't go on a stag night, he starved his entire people.'

. . .

On swine flu: 'It is a tragedy only for people living in slums in Asia or Mexico. But will the honeymoon couple from Edinburgh die? No. A couple of Strepsils will do the job. It's a completely manufactured thing by 24-hour news programmes, taking pictures of people running around in face masks. We have been dealing with swine for many years in the British Airport Authority and the Civil Aviation Authority. And no, we won't be selling face masks on Ryanair.'

. . .

'We should outlaw business-class traffic. We should pack them into economy class rather than have the fat and overpaid flying around on flat beds farting and burping after they've all eaten and drunk their fine wines.'

. . .

'Nobody wants to sit beside a really fat bugger on board. We have been frankly astonished at the number of customers who don't only want to tax fat people but torture them.'

. . .

'BAA should stop buying Noddy train sets which take you halfway round Essex to get you to a satellite building sixty yards away. Our passengers would prefer to walk.'

. . .

'When we used Jet-Way air-bridges, we found that they were the fourth largest cause of delays. If it's raining, passengers will just walk a little faster.'

. . .

'We do not take money. Passengers give it to us voluntarily. This could not be any clearer.'

. . .

'Our most frequent fliers during the summer are people who have large holiday homes in Malaga, Marbella, south of France, Italy, you name it, sending the kids, nannies, gardeners, wives, girlfriends, mistresses up and down on our flights.'

. . .

PLANE SPEAKING

On passengers buying property: 'They should be selling to the people there, not buying from them.

.   .   .

'I would be mystified if anyone is buying a property in France or Spain on the basis that Ryanair gives them a lifetime guarantee of cheap fares. We don't have any obligation to second-home owners that we are always going to carry you there for ever and a day. It's called *caveat emptor*. Please don't ask me to feel sorry for rich people with second homes in France.'

.   .   .

On photo identification: 'We are sorry for the old people who do not have a passport but we cannot include old age pension books as a form of identification. It has to be very simple, which is the reason we require a passport, driving licence or the international student card. We do not want the university card or the Blockbuster video card.'

.   .   .

On a one-hour delay on a flight: 'Three dumb bastards decided they're not going to go to the gate on time. It takes us twice as long to get their bags out of the hold. They should be strung up.'

.   .   .

'Ryanair will never fly the Atlantic route because one cannot get there in a Boeing 737, unless one has a very strong tail wind or passengers who can swim the last hour of the flight.'

.   .   .

'I think half our passengers would like to see me dead and buried, actually, and eventually they'll get what they want. Frankly, I couldn't care less as long as they fly with us.'

.   .   .

'I'm probably just an obnoxious little bollocks. Who cares? The purpose is not to be loved. The purpose is to have the passengers on board.'

FLYING

'For years flying has been the preserve of rich fuckers. Now everyone can afford to fly.'

. . .

'Are we trying to blow up the notion that flying is some kind of orgasmic experience rather than a glorified bus service? Yes, we are. Air transport is just a glorified bus operation. An airplane is nothing more than a bus with wings on.'

. . .

'I think we certainly have democratised flight, in that there's no curtains any more, there's no business class anymore, you're not made to feel, you know, two inches tall, like, "Here you go, down with the poor people at the back." Everybody is the same on Ryanair.'

. . .

'The problem with the airline industry is it is so populated with people who grew up in the 1940s or 1950s who got their excitement looking at airplanes flying overhead. Mercifully I was a child of the 1960s and a trained accountant, so aircraft don't do anything for me.'

. . .

'There's a lot of big egos in this industry. Most chief executives got into this business because they want to travel for a living. Not me, I want to work.'

. . .

'It's a stupid business, which generally loses a lot of money. With the exception of Southwest and ourselves, and easyJet to a lesser extent, nobody makes a lot of money at it.'

. . .

'We'll double the size we are now, unless we do something stupid like have a crash or join an alliance. The biggest threat we face is a management fuck-up, and getting fat and dumb and happy for a couple of years.'

. . .

'Every airline is only as good as its safety record. I am not going to defend our safety because that is almost like denying you beat your wife.'

. . .

PLANE SPEAKING

'I'd love to operate aircraft where we take out the back ten rows and put in hand rails. We'd say if you want to stand, it's five euros. People say, "Oh but the people standing may get killed if there's a crash". Well, with respect, the people sitting down might get killed as well.'

. . .

On travel agents: 'Screw the travel agents. Take the fuckers out and shoot them. They are a waste of bloody time. What have they done for passengers over the years?'

. . .

'We may not be even flying in 2030. We may be all beamed about like *Star Trek*.'

LOW FARES

'Everyone always says, "What's your secret?" It's very simple. Our strategy is like Wal-Mart and Dell. We pile it high and sell it cheap. If anyone beats us on price, we will lower ours.'

. . .

'We are the Tesco of the airline industry. We took the supermarket concept to the skies. Even the unemployed can afford to fly Ryanair.'

. . .

'The low-cost model only really works for short-haul flights. If we started flying farther afield, we'd have to do something stupid, like introducing what I call a "rich class" to make it pay.'

. . .

'The alternative to progress is Thomas Hardy's Wessex: horse-drawn carts, people living below the poverty line and only the very rich going abroad on Italian tours. Now we make it possible for everybody to go on Italian tours.'

. . .

'The car was only liberating in the 1950s for the 5% who could afford them. Nobody moved more than three miles from where they were born. Young people now want to go to Ibiza on bonking holidays. Let them. Ask them in downtown Afghanistan if they would like the M25 and they would bite your hand off.'

. . .

'We're the most profitable airline in the world. We don't do anything that loses money. We don't fly a load of people for £1.99. We might fly 50% of them on a Tuesday in November at £1.99, as it's better than having 50 empty seats. And 25 will buy coffee, 10 a sandwich, one will rent a car. I will make money out of that stuff. We'll take anything to fill flights.'

. . .

'If somebody comes up with a lower fare than us on any route then we will drop our fare straight away. If there's a fare war, we'll start it and we'll finish it.'

. . .

'We have never yet lost money by reducing fares to the travelling public.'

. . .

'I don't see why in 10 years' time you wouldn't fly people for free. Why don't airports pay us for delivering the passengers to their shops?'

. . .

'I'm working on the multiplex model. They make most of their money from the sale of popcorn, drinks and sweets, not from cinema tickets.'

. . .

'All other airlines are asking how they can get up fares. We are asking how can we get rid of them.'

. . .

'I have a vision in the future that we will be flying everyone for free, but I'm damned if I'm going to pay for them to fly.'

. . .

'Price is the best form of loyalty. Ryanair owns price.'

. . .

'Look at all the people who drive for hours to go shopping at Ikea. They don't go there because they think they will come home with a future family heirloom, they go there because it's cheap.'

. . .

If you can't find a low fare on Ryanair: 'You're a moron.'

. . .

'Germans will crawl bollock-naked over broken glass to get low fares.'

IN-FLIGHT

'You want luxury? Go somewhere else.'

. . .

'Anyone who thinks Ryanair flights are some sort of bastion of sanctity where you can contemplate your navel is wrong. We already bombard you with as many in-flight announcements and trolleys as we can. Anyone who looks like sleeping, we wake them up to sell them things.'

. . .

'Don't say it's cheap: that's nasty. The first question 99% of people ask is, "What is your cheapest fare to X?" Nobody asks us about the wine list.'

. . .

'The fact that our tea and coffee supplier is a Fairtrade brand is a welcome bonus, but the decision was based on lowering costs. We'd change to a non-Fairtrade brand in the morning if it was cheaper.'

. . .

'If the drink sales are falling off we get the pilots to engineer a bit of air turbulence. That usually spikes up the drink sales.'

. . .

'At the moment the ice is free, but if we could find a way of targeting a price on it we would.'

. . .

On drinking champagne on Ryanair flights: 'You just have to pay five quid for it.'

. . .

'We don't have the widest seats and you're not getting any free food on board. Bugger off.'

. . .

'We get a surge of complaints the week after the home rugby international against England with fellows writing in: "My good man, I have flown around the world for the last 40 years and I have never been charged for a gin and tonic in my life. I am never flying your appalling, grubby little airline ever again."'

. . .

'We go baggage-handling at the airport once a month in the summer and I never cease to be amazed by the numbers of people who fly in here on €29 and €39 tickets with golf bags the size of cruise missiles and green fee applications where the green fees are €130 to €150.'

. . .

PLANE SPEAKING

'At Stansted, we're now taking different types of people. We even got a complaint from someone in Holland Park. No, it wasn't Richard Branson.'

. . .

'Five years ago one of our engineers realised that we spent €2.5 million repairing reclining seats. How could we not repair them? We took the revolutionary step of going to Boeing and asking for non-reclining seats, so now one of the features of our planes is that they have non-reclining seats.'

. . .

'One of the key glitches we had was security checks, because of those of you who throw the rest of your crap in the seat-back pockets. Well, the cabin crew came up with the legendary idea that we could get rid of the seat-back pockets.'

. . .

On in-flight gambling: 'A lot of people are bored on flights. We believe they have a high propensity to get involved in all sorts of games. We might have the pilot calling out the bingo numbers.'

. . .

On possibly introducing in-flight strip poker: 'I'd pay to see it.'

. . .

On providing in-flight movies: 'We expect it to make enormous sums of money. We wouldn't do it otherwise. Unfortunately, for the moment we think a porn channel is out on taste grounds.'

. . .

On using mobile phones in-flight: 'If you're on a six-hour flight and your bank goes bankrupt you would want to know. We'll have lots of bleating hearts, "Oh, it's very expensive," and yes, it is. Three people around me were sending texts. I was encouraging them, don't just text, make that call.'

. . .

'I was persuaded against my better judgement to put lottery scratch cards on board. I said, "Forget it, they're for morons". After about three months, everybody was scratching lottery cards. So we made more room for scratch cards. If that's what the public wants . . .'

. . .

'We are happy to see families opening up tin-foil packs of sandwiches.'

. . .

'No, we shouldn't give you a bloody cup of coffee. We only charge 19 euros for the ticket.'

. . .

'We recognise your right to object. But good luck, somebody else will have your seat.'

. . .

'We are now thinking about reducing the number of toilets on some of the flights from three to just one. It would mean we could get another six seats on each plane. People may laugh, but it would mean fares would fall by another four per cent.'

. . .

'One thing we have looked at is maybe putting a coin slot on the toilet door so that people might actually have to spend a pound to spend a penny in future. If someone wanted to pay £5 to go to the toilet I would carry them myself. I would wipe their bums for a fiver.'

. . .

'If you look at it sensibly, it would reduce an awful lot of the unnecessary visits to the toilet that pisses so many passengers off on board a plane.'

. . .

'We'll give the money we get for the toilet fees away to some charity for incontinent passengers.'

. . .

'Most people would go to the loo before they get on the plane, or they hold it until they land. It is not likely to happen, but it makes for interesting and very cheap public relations. Boeing can put people on the moon, design fighter aircraft and smart bombs, but they can't design a bloody mechanism to go on doors that will accept coins.'

. . .

'We will charge for every possible thing we can think to charge for, but it will always be the passengers' choice whether they pay it or don't pay it. The suggestion I like best so far is a passenger in Sweden who has suggested that we should produce rolls of toilet paper with my picture on it. I am by some distance the best-looking airline chief executive in Europe.'

BAGGAGE

'Baggage is a throwback to the era of ocean liners. I'd stand on my head if I could fly with an airline and avoid standing in a check-in queue. People are happy to carry a bag onto buses, so why not onto airlines?'

. . .

'Checking-in is the most useless activity known to man. You queue up to hand in your bag and to collect it afterwards – if British Airways hasn't lost your bag, which, 50 per cent of the time, they probably have.'

. . .

'It just needs educating passengers away from this notion that you're going to Klagenfurt for a week and you have to take five bloody suitcases.'

. . .

'Don't complain about checked-in bags. You're the one who checked them in.'

. . .

'We want to get rid of hold baggage. It's one of the biggest costs we have. The average stay of our passengers is less than two days, so the overwhelming majority don't need big bags. If people feel they must take a lot of luggage, they can fly with our higher-fare competitors. If they want to fly round Europe with us for £5 or £10, they will have to do it Ryanair's way.'

. . .

'The purpose is not to make money from checked-in luggage. The purpose is to get rid of it altogether. Will it piss off people who are going on a two-week holiday to Ibiza? Yes, it probably will.'

. . .

On closing Ryanair's check-in desks: 'This isn't the end of civilization as we know it.'

. . .

'When I travel I take only 2 or 3 kg. I can go away for two weeks with just my overnight bag. Instead of packing a hairdryer, why not buy one when you get there?'

. . .

'My wife always takes more than 15kg. I don't know why she needs to pack so much. In fact, on our last flight together, I too was a victim of our excess baggage charge.'

. . .

PLANE SPEAKING

'Passengers are too mentally bloody lazy to travel with carry-on bags. My wife goes away on holidays for a couple of weeks, and she wears bikinis and a few flip-flops, but she needs her 40 pairs of shoes. What do you need 40 pairs of shoes for?'

. . .

On his own carry-on baggage: 'Shirts, more jeans, five pairs of socks and five jocks.'

. . .

On enforcing the company's strict carry-on baggage policy: 'We are not running around like Nazis targeting people. If you turn up at the gate with a bottle of Asti Spumante, all we are saying is, shove it in your bag. I have been a victim of the policy at Gatwick myself when I turned up with a computer bag and a suit bag which was as light as a feather, and it is my own airline.'

CUSTOMER SERVICE

'You're not getting a refund so fuck off.'

. . .

'We are not interested in your sob stories.'

. . .

'Are we going to apologise when something goes wrong? No, we're fucking not. Please understand. It does not matter how many times you write to us complaining that we wouldn't put you up in a hotel because there was fog in Stansted. You didn't pay us for it.'

. . .

'It's unreasonable of passengers to turn up at the airport and expect to be provided with a free cup of tea. People get an apology and the airport restaurant is open. Go and buy a cup of tea yourself.'

. . .

'You'll never find a Ryanair steward pressing a complimentary glass of champagne in your hand.'

. . .

'One will read much of our appalling passenger service.'

. . .

PLANE SPEAKING

'Are we going to say sorry for our lack of customer service? Absolutely not.'

. . .

'Our customers are pretty important. When our customers are wrong then we're not shy about telling them they're wrong. If you show up late for the flight, you're not getting on board the flight.'

. . .

'Our position is simple. Generally speaking, we won't take any phone calls from customers, because they keep you on the bloody phone all day.'

. . .

'Do we occasionally piss people off? Of course we do. But most of the time they're asking for a refund on what everyone knows is a non-refundable ticket.'

. . .

'The way I see it is, when you book a ticket in the UCI cinema and cancel it you don't get a refund, so why should we offer refunds on "non refund" flights?'

. . .

'If you no-show, you've broken the contract and you're not getting any money back.'

. . .

'We don't care if you don't show up.'

. . .

On Kerim Chatty, stopped from boarding a flight due to a gun being found in his bag: 'Of course he's in our passenger figures. We are not going to give him a refund. We are a no-refund airline.'

. . .

'We don't fall over ourselves if you say, "My granny fell ill". What part of "No Refund" don't you understand?'

. . .

'We are bedevilled with a reputation for always being late. In fact, we are always early in comparison to everybody else.'

. . .

On Ryanair coming last in an airline passenger survey: 'You get some obscure website which claims some 4,000 people participated, when it's more like 400 people, and the reality is that you get more publicity in these kinds of surveys by finishing last than first. The respondents were probably all British Airways employees.'

. . .

PLANE SPEAKING

'Our customer service is about the most well-defined in the world. We guarantee to give you the lowest airfare. You get a safe flight. You normally get an on-time flight. That's the package. We don't and won't give you anything more on top of that. We care for our customers in the most fundamental way possible: we don't screw them every time we fly them. Did you get that service? Yes, you did? Fine. Shut up and go away.'

. . .

'Our customer service is unlike every other airline, which has this image of, "We want to fall down at your feet and you can walk all over us and the customer is always right" and all that nonsense.'

. . .

'People will say, as the Founding Fathers wrote down in the American Constitution, we have the inalienable right to bear arms and send in our complaints by e-mail. No, you bloody don't. So go away.'

. . .

'People say the customer is always right, but you know what – they're not. Sometimes they are wrong and they need to be told so.'

. . .

'One of the weaknesses of the company now is it is a bit cheap and cheerful and overly nasty and that reflects my personality.'

'PEACOCKS'

'People ask how we can have such low fares. I tell them our pilots work for nothing.'

.   .   .

'If this is such a Siberian salt mine and I am such an ogre, then why are they still working for the airline? If any of our fellas aren't happy with the current arrangement then they're free to go elsewhere. Godspeed to them.'

.   .   .

'Our pilots are under less pressure because we don't operate to the busiest airports like Heathrow, Charles de Gaulle or Frankfurt. I don't even know how we would put our pilots under pressure. What do you do? Call him up as he's coming in to land?'

.   .   .

'The maximum number of flying hours is 900 a year, divided by 46 weeks: 18 hours a week. Pilots are paid €100,000 a year for flying 18 hours a week. How could you be fatigued working nine days in every two weeks?'

.   .   .

PLANE SPEAKING

'It's quite extraordinary that Ryanair's pilots would fail to accept a five-year pay package which included all captains rising to a salary of £100,000 per annum. They can afford to buy yachts.'

. . .

On charging £50 to those who apply for pilot jobs: 'It's to weed out the timewasters. We had 8,500 applications for 60 jobs and got 600 from people under 16 who didn't even have a driving licence. We're trying to get rid of all the loonies, so from now on if you want to apply you have to pay.'

. . .

On a pilot switching on the Fasten Seat Belts sign to go to the toilet in mid-flight: 'Look, even the captain has to take a leak occasionally. When such times arise, it is normal procedure to switch the seat-belt sign on to ensure all passengers are seated. I agree it's not ideal interrupting customers mid-pee for the captain, but it's all part of ensuring a fast turnaround at the other end.'

. . .

On a Ryanair plane landing at the wrong airport: 'The pilot seems to have made a stupid mistake.'

. . .

On Aer Lingus pilots: 'Overpaid, underworked peacocks.'

. . .

On BALPA, the British Air Line Pilots Association: 'The British Airways Low Pay Association.'

. . .

On the creation of a pan-European Ryanair pilots' association: 'Frankly, the response will be "Piss off". That's spelt P, asterisk, asterisk, asterisk, off.'

. . .

'I don't give a shite if nobody likes me. I am not a cloud bunny, I am not an aerosexual. I don't like aeroplanes. I never wanted to be a pilot like those other platoons of goons who populate the airline industry.'

STAFF

When photographed with several bikini-clad female cabin crew for the launch of the annual staff Charity Calendar: 'We are seriously considering making this the new in-flight uniform.'

. . .

'I enjoyed hearing that I had a complex about what people think of me. I do not give a hoot what people think of me. I care passionately about what people think about Ryanair.'

. . .

'No one can take away the success which the 1,800 people in Ryanair have achieved in recent years. Some would say it is because of me, while many would say it is despite me.'

. . .

'You can't lead 4,000 people in a direction they don't want to go.'

. . .

'We do not have any hard and fast rules on employing new staff on the same terms as existing staff. We do not do any union demarcation bullshit here. We have never had a strike in 20 years because we don't have somebody in the middle telling us lies. We are an embarrassment to a lot of trade unions.'

. . .

'Each of our employees looks after 10,000 passengers per year. In contrast each easyJet employee looks after 6,000 passengers. In BA each employee looks after 800 passengers. But we sub-contract work like baggage handling and our standard aircraft size is bigger than our competitors, so our staff don't work that hard.'

. . .

'We employ 1,800 people - you will get your happy people and your cheesed-off ones.'

. . .

'We use our own biros and I tell the staff not to buy them, just to pick them up from hotels, legal offices, wherever. That's what I do. Recently I did an interview and I was sitting there with a hotel pen I'd nicked from somewhere. I was asked why and I said: 'We at Ryanair have a policy of stealing hotel pens. We won't pay for Bic biros as part of our obsession with low costs.'

. . .

On cancelling a staff Christmas party: 'We wanted people to realise that times are tough, and this sends the message internally that it's a hard world and we cannot be complacent.'

. . .

'A staff pay freeze is a pretty good outcome. If profits were to fall by something like 50 per cent in the next 12 months, it won't be a pay freeze next year, it'll be a pay cut.'

. . .

'I've grown tired of hearing companies say, "People are our greatest asset". We all employ some lazy buggers who need a kick up the backside, but no one can bring themselves to admit it.'

. . .

'MBA students come out with, "My staff is my most important asset." Bullshit. Staff is usually your biggest cost.'

. . .

On how to keep employees motivated and happy:
'Fear.'

AIRCRAFT

'The thing that made Ryanair stand out from the crowd in Europe, instead of being just another shitty European regional airline, was our decision back in 1994 to go with Boeing 737s. And I can't fly the bloody things. I can't even turn them on.'

.   .   .

To Boeing workers in Seattle whilst wearing a RYANAIR LOVES BOEING T-shirt: 'I promise I won't say anything like "Screw Airbus". Bravo Boeing! *Adios* Airbus! The Irish are with you, not those bastards at Airbus. We have rejected them. They are crap. I will do *Riverdance*.'

.   .   .

'Boeing made a lot of bullshit promises in 1999, but uniquely in the history of aviation they have beaten them. This is the best bloody aircraft in the world for short-haul operations. You people build the best god-damn aircraft in the world. My three favourite words are "Made in Seattle".'

.   .   .

PLANE SPEAKING

'The message to Boeing today is: "You keep building them, we'll keep buying them", and together both of us will kick the crap out of Airbus in Europe. We love Boeing. Fuck the French.'

.   .   .

'The Irish built most of the roads in America and most of the railways in America until the Chinese came along and undercut us and we are confident we will build the biggest scheduled airline in Europe with Boeing's help.'

.   .   .

On ordering new aircraft from Boeing at half price:
'One of many natural advantages I have is that I grew up in Mullingar, and farmers know that the time to buy is when everyone else is selling and the time to sell is when everyone else is buying. So we went and bought up about two years' worth of production. We raped them. I wouldn't even tell my priest what discount I got.'

.   .   .

On announcing a large aircraft order beside David Bonderman, Chairman of Ryanair: 'He's a lot richer than me, and we need the guy with the big cheque book to show up for the big-ticket items.'

.   .   .

On offering advice to the boss of Air Asia: 'Just fucking buy Boeing.'

. . .

'Ryanair will never fly two types of aircraft, but that's not to say we would never switch. It would take a few years to make a smooth changeover, but if it made sense we'd do it without hesitation.'

. . .

On the Airbus A320: 'I've heard a lot of horseshit about a wider fuselage. I've yet in 15 years in this industry to meet one passenger who booked his ticket based on that.'

. . .

On not ordering more aircraft from Boeing: 'Boeing had their chance. Eventually you lose interest, dealing with a bunch of idiots who can't make a decision. They are a bunch of numpties out in Seattle.'

HISTORY

'I started to work for Tony Ryan in 1987 and that is how I got into aviation. Tony Ryan is a genius. I learnt an awful lot from him. You get few opportunities in life to learn from someone so rich and successful. Everybody else was worried about the cost of women's knickers and the cost of this, that and the other, but Tony had maps of the world looking at where he could lease aircraft.'

. . .

'I couldn't get a real job. It just sort of fell out of the sky. My title was bag man. I was based on his farm in Tipperary - the job was anything from hunting cattle, running errands, doing tax returns.'

. . .

'They lost the run of themselves. Tony has never been a great man to focus on cost. He wanted it to be elegant, to deliver a better service, business class and frequent flyer club; I mean complete bloody nonsense, to serve nice china mugs and slippers but charge ten quid. You can decide to either be Marks & Spencer or be Fortnum & Mason but you can't be something in between.'

. . .

'When I first arrived at Ryanair it was like you'd arrived at the pearly gates. There was a gorgeous blonde chick at every desk. The place was a shambles, yet it was still amazingly sexy.'

'Ryanair was set up originally to take on Aer Lingus and British Airways on the Dublin to London route and offer low fares, but they kind of lost the plot a bit. They were opening routes fucking left, right and centre, the route network was nuts. They had no fucking schedule at all.'

. . .

'We were trying to do what many other airlines were trying to do in Europe, which was to be a slightly lower fare "me too" carrier to Aer Lingus or British Airways. But the fares were about 20 per cent cheaper, which meant we just lost more money than they did.'

. . .

'The accounts were rubbish. There was nobody collecting cash. We didn't know how much money we had, except that we had nothing in the bank. The bottom line was that if Tony Ryan didn't give us a million quid by next Friday we couldn't pay the wages.'

. . .

'It was very high profile. I didn't want a high profile. I wanted to make lots of money but not be known. That was the way my family would operate, there was no credit for being in the papers.'

. . .

'My role in Ryanair from 1988 to 1991 was to stop it losing money - it wasn't looking to make Tony Ryan money. We were hovering on the verge of bankruptcy. In Spring 1991 I thought it would be a miracle if we were still in business three months later.'

'I thought in a good year we'd make a couple of million and I'd get £250,000, and there you go, more money than I could imagine, I'd be rich. But at that stage it was as likely to go bust as it was to make a million quid.'

. . .

'Over two or three years three of us together did turn the airline around and put it on the footing it is on today. I get far too much credit for being the turnaround artist.'

. . .

'I didn't particularly want a job in the company that I was recommending should be closed down.'

. . .

'I said, close the fucking airline because it's a basket case. Eventually we made a £10 million profit and the Ryans had to write me a cheque for £3.5 million, at which point they said "Hang on".

. . .

'I spent from age 20 to 40 working like a black. I can bloody say that.'

. . .

'Ryanair will never make money. It will always lose money. It's an airline. Forget it.'

. . .

'I joined as a toilet cleaner and I'm still shovelling shit.'

PRESENT DAY

'Our strategy is about running the airline the way people want. There are only three layers of management. No dogma. No unions. I drive buses at the airport, check in passengers, load bags and get a good kicking when I play for the baggage handlers' football team.'

. . .

'We can fly six aircraft a day where Aer Lingus or British Airways could fly four. Where they can get six in the air, we fly eight. So we're 20-25 per cent more efficient from the very start. It's so simple a four-year-old could work it out.'

. . .

'Some airlines enter a new route and aim to make a profit in three years. We will not enter a route if we cannot break even in three hours and grow the market by at least one hundred per cent.'

. . .

'We are growing like gangbusters. There is an almost insatiable demand for low-fare air travel.'

. . .

'Ryanair is going to be a monster in Europe in the next ten to twelve years.'

. . .

'We are up to our goolies at the moment in work.'

. . .

'A story circulated that we were banning people from charging their mobile phones in the office, saving ourselves 0.00002 cents per day. I issued a press release saying that, absolutely, we ban mobile phone charging. The more we can sound nasty, petty and cheap, the more we can reinforce in people's minds that we are extremely bloody cheap and they will choose to fly with us.'

. . .

'We would welcome a good, deep recession for 12-18 months. During recessions travel does not get cut back but people look for cheaper alternatives. If we get a recession I don't see people cutting back on the amount of flying. A little bit of recession would be very good for the economy.'

. . .

'Jesus, we don't look bright. If we were bright we wouldn't be working for airlines. We're no experts on oil prices here. Frankly, we'll never get it right. It's an inability to hedge properly.'

. . .

'We would have done better if we had waited another week. If oil keeps falling we have done a bad job. If anyone shoots someone and the oil price goes back up then we've done a good job.'

'Oil may run out in the year 2150 or 2200. You won't be here. I won't be here. Frankly I don't care.'

. . .

'It is much more fun when the world is falling apart than when things are boring and going well.'

. . .

On the biggest risk to Ryanair's future growth: 'Me. Management indiscipline. If we get sloppy, start winning awards, pontificating, writing books, building new headquarters, dating pop stars - sorry, that's OK - then I think we're dead. Or the danger is that we screw this up ourselves, like the chief executive writes a book on how to run airlines. Then we're really screwed.'

. . .

On how Ryanair might fail: 'Nuclear war in Europe, an accident by ourselves or some other low fares carrier in Europe or believing our own bullshit.'

. . .

'The only thing I will not do is fly the aircraft.'

. . .

'My role in making Ryanair succeed is to interfere as little as possible, try to stay out of other people's way and then claim the credit for all the success when it comes along.'

INVESTORS

On beginning a press conference to announce the annual results: 'I'm here with Howard Millar and Michael Cawley, our two deputy-chief executives. But they're presently making love in the gentlemen's toilets, such is their excitement at today's results.'

. . .

'The word "profitability" is often portrayed as a dirty word here but I fail to see why one is in business if one is not in business to make money.'

. . .

'There is a lot of bullshit out there and to be honest I don't know where it is coming from.'

. . .

'This will be my first and last speech.'

. . .

'People look at 20 per cent profit margins in the airline business and they assume you are smuggling drugs or doing something naughty with the figures.'

. . .

'Any idiot can paint a plane and start out offering low fares. It's about sustainability.'

. . .

'We expect our profits to grow by 20 to 25 per cent. That's not just good, that's practically obscene in an industry in which few people make money. This isn't an airline, it's a drug baron's business.'

. . .

'These are very good numbers. We have a very highly rated share at the moment, but at the end of the day we want everyone to remember it's an airline and not some kind of technology stock.'

. . .

'Our stock price jumped up. I think we closed today at €8.80. It takes analysts a while to digest things. If they had a good understanding of the business they would not be analysts.'

. . .

On his company accounts: 'It's perfectly straightforward. EBITDA? That's some bloody number I don't understand.'

. . .

At a press conference to float Ryanair: 'You're probably wondering why we're suddenly talking to everybody for the first time in ten years. When this is finished we'll probably disappear for another ten years.'

. . .

'We would love to have a woman on our board. One of our most senior people, Caroline Green, and I don't mean to be politically incorrect here, is obviously a woman. But we are not putting a woman on our board just to cover our arse.'

. . .

'We are never paying a dividend as long as I live and breathe and as long as I'm the largest individual shareholder. If you are stupid enough to invest in an airline for its dividend flow you should be put back in the loony bin where you came from. There's no reliable stream for a dividend.'

'We'll be looking at very substantial senior management bonuses and distributions to shareholders, in that order. I think I'm worth it.'

. . .

After a Ryanair profits warning: 'Hey, live with it. Remember Tesco had a drop in profits four years ago and nobody said its business model was bust.'

. . .

'Screw the share price. We're in a fares war. I own more of the shares than anyone else. They can join the queue behind me. If they are not happy they can always sell their shares.'

. . .

'There is absolutely no harm in losing the mythical horseshit that we can walk on water. Given that this is our first profits warning, the market went nuts. But there is no point whingeing that everybody has got it in for us. Perhaps we deserved a slap around the head.'

. . .

'Any chief executive who doesn't have a sense of their own mortality is heading for disaster. They read articles describing themselves as visionaries and geniuses. They shouldn't believe it any more than when the press are calling them gobshites and wankers.'

CORPORATE LIFE

'Business is simple. You buy it for this, you sell it for that, and the bit in the middle is ultimately your profit or loss.'

. . :

'The meek may inherit the earth, but they will not have it for long.'

. . .

'We don't bluster. We make threats and carry them out.'

. . .

'The downside of success that we really worry about is the danger that the more successful you are, the more likely you are to lose sight of the things that made you successful.'

. . .

'Having a long-term plan is a waste of time. I'm not a thinker. You see opportunities and you try to take them. There's no point having some long term plan because a long-term plan gets knocked on its ass.'

. . .

'You won't get anywhere settling for mediocrity or simply getting by.'

. . .

'There's an awful lot of bullshit talked about brands. Ryanair is a pretty good, anodyne brand that works across Europe. We have no intention of changing the brand or redesigning the image or the rest of that old nonsense. In my thirteen years at this company, British Airways has changed three times. We've not changed it once, and the virtue of what we've done has been proven.'

. . .

On corporate governance: 'Those are the kinds of questions you ask companies that are about to go bankrupt, not one that is making more than €200 million a year in profit and has €1.1 billion in cash.'

. . .

On Enron: 'At Ryanair everything is on the balance sheet. Ryanair has not succumbed to Enronitis. For the ninth year on the trot our net margin actual profits after tax is 21 per cent and that does not go into my pocket, where I think it belongs, but onto the balance sheet.'

. . .

On advertising agencies: 'They were all the same. They were 40-year-old men with ponytails, black suits, black t-shirts and a big buckle on their belt.'

. . .

On consultants: 'I believe hiring consultants is an abdication by management of their responsibilities. If the consultant is so good at managing change, then why not hire him to run the company and do it himself? Every idiot who gets fired in the industry shows up as a consultant somewhere. I would shoot any consultant who came through my door.'

'Business books are bullshit and are usually written by wankers.'

On not using email: 'My inbox just fills up with shite. I couldn't be bothered with all the crud and the crap and the rubbish that gets sent to you on e-mails.'

On being branded the 'unacceptable face of capitalism': 'It's a title I won proudly.'

. . .

On winning the European Business Campaigner of the Year award: 'Business Campaigner? More like Business Complainer of the Year.'

. . .

On being named by financial magazine *Barron's* as one of the 'world's most respected CEOs': 'Barf!'

. . .

On winning a Business Leader of the Year Award: 'I am deeply humbled, but surely we are doomed. There are three signs you need to be wary of when looking at a business - when it buys a helicopter, moves into plush new headquarters and when it wins awards. It usually tends to lead to complacency in the company or from the gobshite who wins it. But I was a gobshite anyway.'

'ECO-NUTS'

'It's July, the press have nothing to write about. The Prime Minister's on holiday, the World Cup is over, Zidane has retired - I know, let's write about the impact of aviation on the environment.'

. . .

'The BBC runs green week, ITV runs greener week, Sky runs even greener week, Channel 4 runs even bloody greener week and each time they use a picture of aircraft taking off.'

. . .

On Sir Nicolas Stern's climate change report: 'There's a lot of misinformation and lies being put about by the eco-nuts in this country. If you listen to them you would think aviation was responsible for melting the polar ice caps, heating up the globe by two per cent a year and for every war, pestilence and the SARS epidemic.'

. . .

'I don't think the advice of a bunch of UN scientists should be taken as gospel truth.'

. . .

'The sustainable aviation group, God help us, is another bunch of lemmings shuffling towards a cliff edge. A lot of members of the sustainable aviation group won't be around in ten years' time. That'll be their main contribution to sustainable aviation.'

. . .

'We want to annoy the fuckers whenever we can. The best thing we can do with environmentalists is shoot them. These headbangers want to make air travel the preserve of the rich. They are Luddites marching us back to the 18th century. If preserving the environment means stopping poor people flying so only the rich can fly, then screw it.'

. . .

'I listen to all this drivel about turning down the central heating, going back to candles, returning to the dark ages. You do that if you want to. But none of it will make any difference.'

. . .

'If you're concerned about the environment, stop driving.'

. . .

'The chattering bloody classes, or what I call the liberal *Guardian* readers, they're all buying SUVs to drive around London. I smile at these loons who drive their SUVs down to Sainsbury's and buy kiwi fruit from New Zealand. They're flown in from New Zealand for Christ sakes. They're the equivalent of environmental nuclear bombs! But nobody says, "Let's ban the kiwi fruits".'

. . .

'Why aren't they whacking a huge tax on bananas and grapes flown in from half way round the world? Why don't they eat British turnips all winter if they want to save air flights? Because they can't live without their scallops from Chile.'

. . .

'The Swampies of this world are climbing up trees to protest about airlines and airports. They should all get a job and get a fucking life.'

. . .

'If everybody stopped flying for the next 12 months and CO_2 levels fell by 2%, it would represent less than the oil- and coal-fired stations to be opened by the Chinese in the next 12 months.'

. . .

'Soon it won't matter how many lights we turn off or how many bicycles we ride or flights we take, the damage will have been done on the other side of the world by a billion people in China and India who have only just discovered the delights of turning on lights.'

. . .

'The point is you can't change the world by putting on a pair of dungarees or sandals.'

. . .

'Human breathing is one of the biggest problems as far as I can see, so why don't the environmentalists just shoot all the humans?'

. . .

'Let's go nuclear if you really want to do something and then let's watch the eco-nuts go crazy.'

. . .

'I did not suggest that we shoot cows. I simply offered the factual information that since they generated greater emissions than global aviation, perhaps some of these eco-warriors would expect us to shoot all farm animals in pursuit of their misguided, inaccurate and misinformed agenda.'

. . .

'Emissions is a load of bollocks talked up by all these sandal-wearing greens and other headbangers, most of whom fly on Ryanair when they go to protest at G8 meetings. It's a lot of hot air.'

. . .

'I don't think emissions credit trading will come in. How are you going to get the Italians to pay?'

. . .

'Gordon Brown wants us all to believe that he spends his days mulching his compost with his children. David Cameron's gone Dutch with his windmills and clogs. Neither of them really means it. They know that changing a light bulb isn't going to make any difference, but a picture of them changing a light bulb will be a nice, cosy image.'

. . .

'Gordon Brown's proposals won't stop people flying, petrol tax doesn't stop us driving. They are all stealth taxes. The Chancellor is just lying when he says these new taxes are environmental. Mr Brown is not even a light shade of khaki.'

. . .

On the Bishop of London, who said it was sinful to pollute the planet by jetting away on holiday: 'The Bishop of London has got empty churches - presumably if no one went on holiday perhaps they might turn up and listen to his sermons. God bless the bishop. The bishops have got their own crosses to bear. Goodness knows what he would know about greenhouse gases. He was obviously at some dinner party with the chatterati. It's the usual clichéd horseshit that we hear.'

. . .

'To suggest that I and Ryanair do not have regard to the environment is clearly untrue and damaging to Ryanair's good name and reputation.'

. . .

'The skies are empty. I say keep flying.'

. . .

'There is no relationship between the aviation industry and climate change and global warming.'

. . .

'Why don't I support anything that increases the cost of flying? Because I run an airline. Why are we all rolling around pulling wool out of our navels about cheap flights in the UK?'

. . .

'Aircraft emissions are less than marine transport, and yet I don't see anyone saying, you know, "Let's tax the fuck out of the ferries".'

. . .

'Trains are incredibly over-subsidised and don't service people's needs. The trains were fine in Victorian times when if you didn't have a stable you walked, but no one needs to use them now.'

. . .

'We will go from 40 to 80 million passengers in the next few years. We will take them off British Airways and the other old carriers who are flying gas-guzzling, ancient aircraft and pack them into fuel efficient planes. So Ryanair will be saving the environment - not that we care much.'

. . .

'If the climate heated up by a couple of degrees, Ireland could have a nice Mediterranean climate.'

. . .

'Talk is cheap – free, in fact. And it makes people feel better. But the reality is ... look out of the window, what do you see? Rain. It's pissing rain. This is the middle of August. Climate change is not the biggest threat to mankind. If it is, why is the summer so crappy?'

SECURITY

'Generally, the best time to visit anywhere is after a terrorist attack because the hotels are discounting like mad and the place is crawling with security.'

. . .

After the events of 9/11: 'We're in the shit now. How are we going to dig our way out of it? We've had record bookings over this weekend. We're not going to be put out of business by a bunch of terrorists.'

. . .

'You might be scared of flying at £200 return, but you'll be a lot less scared flying at £20 return.'

. . .

On the Foot and Mouth emergency: 'If you took the decision to buy a non-refundable ticket and did not take out travel insurance, please don't come to us asking us to be the insurer of last resort because, I promise you, we have our own problems at the moment.'

. . .

On extra UK security measures: 'These are farcical Keystone Cops security measures that don't add anything except to block up airports. These measures are giving the terrorists and extremists an unbelievable public relations success. We are not going to die at the hands of toiletries. We shall fight them on the beaches, we shall fight them in the air, we shall fight them with toiletries.'

. . .

'Laurel and bloody Hardy are working at the Department of Transport coming up with these security measures.'

. . .

'The Noddies in the Home Office decided they'd got some intelligence that lipstick was the new weapon of mass destruction: that Osama bin Laden had spent years in a cave developing a range of lipsticks unknown to Estée Lauder, which were the new weapons of mass destruction. It's been a weapon of man's destruction for a couple of centuries, but that's another matter.'

. . .

'Searching terrorist suspects like five- and six-year-children travelling with their parents and elderly people in wheelchairs going to Spain on holidays who are clearly potentially a great threat to the great British public will have the terrorists laughing in the caves in Pakistan.'

. . .

PLANE SPEAKING

'You don't see the government confiscating lipsticks and gel-filled bras on the London Underground. Most of them couldn't identify a gel-filled bra if it jumped up and bit them anyway.

. . .

On a bomb scare in Scotland: 'The police force were outstanding in their field. But all they did was stand in their field. They kept passengers on board while they played with a suspect package for two and three quarter hours. Extraordinary.'

. . .

On a Sunday afternoon when only 7 out of 14 security check points at Stansted were manned: 'The only explanation was that Arsenal and Tottenham Hotspur were both playing football on the television and there were huge no-shows among security staff because many of them live in North London. We have written to the Football League asking them not to schedule Arsenal and Spurs matches on the same Sunday afternoon.'

. . .

'Air marshals are a complete waste of time.
I can't think of anything that would reduce security more than having a guy on board with a gun.'

POLITICIANS

'I upset a lot of people because I tell them what I think. I'm disrespectful towards what is perceived to be authority. Like, I think the Prime Minister of Ireland is a gobshite.'

. . .

'It's called democracy. If the Prime Minister is incompetent or doing a shit job, I or every other citizen of this country is free to call him a spineless tosser, which is what he is.'

. . .

'Nobody ever takes on governments. Everyone wants to work their way round them with influence and lobbying. Why not shout the bastards down?'

. . .

'In politics you have to pander to all these vested interests, and tell people what they want to hear. I don't have the patience for that. I tell people what I think - which is usually what they don't want to hear. If I went to run for politics, the trade unions would go apoplectic.'

. . .

'What makes you successful in business ultimately dooms you to failure in politics. Business is about being tough, decisive and leading from the front.'

. . .

PLANE SPEAKING

'Unlike politicians we don't accept cash - only credit cards.'

. . .

'I have never yet come across a politician who will make a political decision in your favour or against your favour unless it was in their interest, or in what they consider to be the national interest. They just don't make decisions based on the fact that you sponsored something, or that they stayed in some holiday home of yours.'

. . .

'I think the most influential person in Europe in the last 20 to 30 years has been Margaret Thatcher, who has left a lasting legacy that has driven us towards lower taxes and greater efficiency. Without her we'd all be living in some French bloody inefficient unemployed republic.'

. . .

On the Lisbon Treaty: 'Yes I have read the Treaty. It is a fucking pain in the arse of a document. I nearly died of boredom from reading it. Vote Yes because it's the fucking sensible thing to do.'

. . .

On flying Tony Blair on his holidays to Carcassonne: 'The savings the Blair family made flying with us compared to flying with British Airways to Toulouse were in excess of £2,000. Even very rich people, who may be travelling with four or five children and a nanny, are turning to us to save money. Even Tony Blair doesn't get paid enough for British Airways fares.'

. . .

'People may pretend they don't fly Ryanair but everyone does it. Tony Blair, half the Royal Family. If I showed you our passenger list, we'd have half the House of Lords, lots of MPs. The chatterati hate mass tourism but they travel with us to their Italian villas. They all love a bargain.'

. . .

'Gordon Brown raised taxes on airlines. It has fuck all to do with climate change. Some of these guilt-laden, middle-class liberals think it's somehow good: "Oh, that's my contribution to the environment." It's not. You're just being robbed. It's just highway fucking robbery.'

. . .

'The weather's rubbish and so is the cricket. People want a couple of weeks in the sun. The only people I know who are "stay-cationing" are boring buggers like Gordon Brown.'

. . .

'Gordon Brown is only staying in Britain because he is too frightened that if he leaves someone will nick his job. It's just government by poll and spin-doctor. Thatcher and Blair didn't dither.'

. . .

'If I were David Cameron I would stop competing over who is better at riding a bicycle and call for a serious debate on the next generation of nuclear power stations. Sticking a windmill on top of your house is not the answer.'

. . .

'David Cameron may be holidaying in Cornwall but he flew halfway around the world just to see some huskies. David Cameron can hug trees because he won't have to do much to get into power, but it is not a way to run a country.'

. . .

'The UK needs a new government because they are a group of witless, hopeless Scots whose solution to the recession is to tax your way out. If that was the answer Ted Heath would have been elected for six successive terms.'

THE EUROPEAN COMMISSION

'Consumers have been ripped off for the past fifty years because governments got together with the airlines after 1945. British Airways got the monopoly in the UK, Air France the monopoly in France and Lufthansa the monopoly in Germany. The airline industry is the only industry where the producers are allowed by the idiots in Brussels to get together once or twice a year to fix the fares and route capacities and they get anti-trust immunity to do it. It's a joke.'

. . .

'I think we should blow the place up and shoot all the regulators and the airline business might actually prosper. I've no intention of making life easy for bureaucrats.'

. . .

'It's fun to challenge the European Commission because they are politically corrupt.'

. . .

'Sometimes it's good to show Brussels the two fingers.'

. . .

PLANE SPEAKING

'We're not paranoid but Brussels really do have it in for us.'

. . .

'I believe these morons in the European Commission are making air travel more expensive, but I wouldn't be interested in sitting down trying to educate a bunch of civil servants.'

. . .

On an EU investigation into subsidies at Charleroi Airport: 'Someone here is looking for a smoking gun and there isn't one. We haven't received a letter from the EU, but if we do I think it would get a pretty short reply. I think it would consist of two words; Foxtrot Oscar. We spent over a hundred million euros building the bloody base. So our reply will say, we're paying nothing, love Mick.'

. . .

On an adverse EU ruling on Charleroi Airport: 'It's a complete fuck-up which is going to overturn twenty years of competition in air travel, but it wouldn't be the first time the EU has made a balls of an investigation. The judgement is just blindingly wrong. There will be a repayment over my dead body. We have written back to say fuck off.'

. . .

'There are fucking Kim Il-Jungs in the Commission. You cannot have civil servants trying to design rules that make everything a level playing field. That's called North fucking Korea, and everybody is starving there. The EU are pursuing some form of communist fucking Valhalla.'

. . .

'Are we the good guys? Absolutely. Are the commission the bad guys? They are the evil empire if this is the kind of decision they come up with. Brussels is the centre of communist Europe.'

. . .

'Would it have made a difference if anyone else had made the case to Brussels? No. It wouldn't matter who it was with those Communists on the Commission. Zey are Communists, numbnuts, bureaucrats. Ve vill fight zem in ze hills, ve vill fight zem on ze beaches, ve vill neverrrr zurrenderr. Our lawyers are so confident of winning it on appeal, I'm worried.'

. . .

'Why should a Wal-Mart located outside a city centre, for example, pay the same rent as those in city-centre locations? It's like saying that Wal-Mart will only get the same discounts as the corner grocery store, and if Wal-Mart ask for any discounts on bigger volumes they will be told no. All we received were discounts, just like Tesco would receive from its cheese suppliers.'

. . .

'Some people love the idea that the Charleroi decision is going to end low-cost air travel for ever. It isn't - we are an unstoppable force.'

. . .

'We're not going to let this one drop, and we'll be off to every European court in every hill and valley. We will never surrender. The commission's decision on Charleroi is crucial. It will be our Waterloo and we will win it. We will sue the arse off the Commission.'

. . .

'We will lose a lot of these cases, then win them all on appeal. Our appeal is a legal case: it won't require lobbying politicians, who are as useful as condom in a convent.'

. . .

'Given our outstanding record with legal actions we're very confident we'll be successful. So far the tally's running at 99 losses and 2 wins.'

. . .

'We've got €1.2 billion in cash. The interest from next week's deposit will pay whatever the bloody fine is. The issue here is the principle.'

. . .

On European air-traffic control: 'Deregulate and privatise the fuckers and let them compete.'

. . .

'Air traffic control can walk out any time they like and no one gets compensation. Public officials shouldn't be able to go on strike. They can't be sacked, so there should be some quid pro quo.'

. . .

'I don't give a damn about labour laws in France. We'll break the laws in France if that's what needs to be done.'

. . .

On EU Commissioner Neelie Kroes' approval of an Alitalia/Air One merger: 'She'll be rolling over like a poodle having her tummy tickled and rubber-stamping the thing.'

. . .

'We will be complying with European legislation pledging compensation for passenger delays but not embracing them. It's a lot of rubbish. They will get overturned in the end. It's stupid legislation but that is what Brussels does. Most claims will be met with "Not our fault, go away". It's just a bullshit piece of legislation and it won't survive a case in the European Court.'

. . .

'It would be easier for a camel to pass through the eye of a needle than for Ryanair to get a fair hearing in Brussels.'

'BA-STARDS'

'Businessmen need to stop drinking champagne at six o'clock in the morning on British Airways flights. They need to get there on time. Why the hell would anyone fly with BA and pay four or five hundred quid just to be late?'

. . .

'The idea that you get on board a seven o'clock flight from Brussels to Frankfurt and you get some inedible breakfast and two screw-top bottles of Champagne that you can't drink anyway, that's over. [Name of top chef deleted] will cook you a meal and reheat it five times so it tastes like a load of mush.'

. . .

'British Airways are skyway robbery. They are expensive BA-stards.'

. . .

On BA passengers stranded in a BA strike: 'This punctured the myth that BA has tried to perpetuate that if something goes wrong BA will look after you. Thousands of BA's high-fares passengers are left to sleep on the terminal floor with no free food, no free drinks and no hotel accommodation. They left the passengers in the terminal for the weekend. By the way, we probably would too if we had that bad a weekend. You can't buy 80,000 hotel rooms.'

. . .

'On British Airways, your luggage will travel further than you will.'

. . .

On cancelling a £900 ticket on British Airways, booked by his bankers, in preference for a £59 ticket on his own airline: 'It just shows you how banks piss away money. No, I didn't get a £59 fare because I'm the chief executive, anyone could have booked with us today and got that fare.'

. . .

'BA said they would introduce new uniforms. It's back to the Fifties, which is where most of these muttonheads' thinking is. If fine wine and food don't get you and Heathrow doesn't persuade you, now you have got shorter skirts to attract you back to BA and its £200 average fares.'

. . .

'If I were the chief executive of BA, I would give up.'

. . .

'If I was Willie Walsh, I'd have my CV out there looking for another job.'

. . .

'BA have got waterfalls in their head office. The first thing I'd do if I were in charge of BA is turn off the waterfalls. The only time we have waterfalls in the Ryanair office is when the toilet or the sink leaks.'

. . .

PLANE SPEAKING

On the British Airways / Iberia merger: 'It reminds me of two drunks leaning on each other.'

. . .

'British Airways won't be growing its existing emission levels because it's going nowhere - it's shrinking. A move to the moon might be needed to streamline British Airway's operations.'

. . .

'There is too much "We really admire our competitors". All bollocks. Everyone wants to kick the shit out of everyone else. We want to beat the crap out of British Airways. They mean to kick the crap out of us.'

. . .

'We love tilting at the English, have done it for about 700 years, but we're only getting our own back. Remember you beat the crap out of us for the first 600 years.'

. . .

On his recreations as listed in *Who's Who:* 'BA-bashing.'

. . .

'Do you know how many people British Airways has in its customer services department? 200. Do you know how many we have? Four.'

. . .

'BA will become the first company in economic history to make money by selling fewer things to fewer people at lower prices. It has no chance of working.'

. . .

'Go to BA headquarters and tell the CEO he's going to grow profits by 12 per cent this year and he'd have an orgasm. I say, God speed. You're doing an outstanding job. Keep it up.'

. . .

'We don't need BA to fall over itself for us to succeed. It's been falling over for the last five years.'

. . .

'A Mickey Mouse Irish airline can start in a field in Waterford and in 20 years the self-styled, self-proclaimed world's favourite airline is overtaken by the world's lowest price airline. Now there's a thing.'

. . .

'We're asking British Airways whether they are prepared to give their "world's favourite airline" tag to a poor bunch of Paddies. We are going to borrow the BA advertising slogan as "the world's favourite airline", put a line through BA and say "Oh no you're not - the Paddies are".

. . .

'I see myself as a jumped-up Paddy running a good airline that gives great fares and screws BA.'

. . .

'Eventually there'll be one last British Airways flight with a bunch of old toffee-nosed snobs on it but all the kids of the toffee-nosed snobs will be flying on Ryanair.'

EASYJET

On the founder of easyJet: 'There are very few examples of where I would follow Stelios in anything. He's Greek and I'm Irish. The Greeks will never outdo the Irish in anything. We'll even outdo them in drinking. He's the son of a billionaire. He could have been a rich tosser, but at least he did something and set up an airline.'

. . .

'It will be a cold day in hell before the Greeks get one over the Irish. They're welcome to have a go but they'll get a kickback.'

. . .

'Ryanair was the first low fares / no frills airline in Europe, and the first low fares / no frills route was flying from the UK seven years before easyJet started. Whatever Stelios and easyJet may have done, they certainly weren't the first or the founders - Ryanair was.'

. . .

On the founder of easyJet: 'Those of us who sell the lowest air fares just get on with it, and those who do not, write whingeing letters to newspapers.'

. . .

'easyJet are not the brightest sandwiches in the picnic basket.'

. . .

When easyJet bought the British Airways subsidiary Go: 'Embarking on an acquisition of another higher fare airline at this time is certainly a ballsy move. I will be taking lessons in humility now that we are, for the time being, Europe's second-largest low-fares airline.'

. . .

'We want to eliminate the idea that EasyJet is somehow a low-cost carrier. It isn't. Its average fares are 70% higher than ours. It's time to sort out who is the low-fare airline. It is Ryanair. It is not easyJet. They are a medium-fare airline.'

. . .

When sitting and wearing army combat fatigues on a WWII tank outside easyJet's headquarters at Luton Airport: 'I've been told and it's no lie, easyJet's fares are way too high. It's about peace, not war. We want a piece of British Airways, a piece of Lufthansa and a piece of easyJet.'

. . .

'There's scope for easyJet to be a profitable airline competing with the numbnuts in Europe as long as they stay out of our way.'

.   .   .

'easyJet are a convenient target for us to have a go at, but they do what they do, and we do what we do, but we do it that much better.'

.   .   .

'The future is not about the competition between Ryanair and easyJet because with the greatest respect that competition is over. Eventually easyJet will lose to Ryanair because we have a lower cost base. They are British Midland Mark 2.'

OTHER AIRLINES

'We went to look at Southwest Airlines in the US. It was like the road to Damascus. This was the way to make Ryanair work. I met with Herb Kelleher. I passed out about midnight, and when I woke up again at about 3 a.m. Kelleher was still there, the bastard, pouring himself another bourbon. I thought I'd pick his brains and come away with the Holy Grail. The next day I couldn't remember a thing.'

. . .

'Southwest was a big guiding thing for me, banging aircraft out after fifteen minutes. They were phenomenal, passengers loved it. I saw it with my own eyes and said, "We can do this in Europe".'

. . .

'How important is Herb Kelleher? The man is a genius. Herb Kelleher is like God. All we've done is copy Herb Kelleher's successful model.'

. . .

'I think Southwest should have taken Herb out and shot him about 10 years ago.'

. . .

'We like to think in Ryanair we have a number of traits in common with Southwest. Firstly it's run by the drunken Irish, and we like to pride ourselves on our ability to party, and fly while over the limit. Secondly the Irish and Texans have a number of other things in common, like humility, religion and gun laws.'

. . .

On Aer Lingus being named best-value airline in Europe in a survey: 'In reality Aer Lingus have won an award for ripping people off by slightly less than they were ripping people off years ago.'

. . .

'In the last four weeks Aer Lingus management appear to have made little progress on their cost reduction plan, beyond changing its name. Their "customer-driven plan with a clear business focus" is Japanese for higher fares.'

. . .

'Aer Lingus has an interesting approach to fuel surcharges in that it does not impose them on the short-haul routes but on the long-haul routes it now adds a surcharge of €100 a ticket. Its explanation is that somehow long-haul flying is different from short-haul flying because on short-haul one is flying on Coca-Cola or something, whereas on long-haul one is flying on jet kerosene.'

. . .

On whether a large loss on Aer Lingus shares was a good investment by Ryanair: 'Yes, and you can attribute that to Ryanair's largest individual shareholder. It has been mentioned by our shareholders; the response was two words, and the second word was "off". The €300m invested by Ryanair in Aer Lingus is just a drop in the ocean. This isn't a lot of money. I sit in front of our shareholders and say, 'I own more shares in the company than you do, now fuck off.'

. . .

On buying a stake in Aer Lingus: 'It was a stupid investment. I never say sorry, except to my wife who I apologise to all the time.'

. . .

'The chief executive of Lufthansa says Germans don't like low fares. How the fuck does he know? He's never offered them any. He is eighteen months behind the times.'

. . .

'If €99 fares is the best Lufthansa can do for the World Cup then they shouldn't bother leaving the changing rooms. Their €99 fares are own goals. I feel like the Michael Owen of the airline industry, beating the Germans on their home turf.'

. . .

PLANE SPEAKING

'Lufthansa in Germany makes even British Airways look cheap. We are stuffing it to Lufty. I'd like to thank Lufthansa for their help setting us up in Germany.'

. . .

'The only thing that Lufthansa have not yet got is an injunction on from the German courts to prevent Ryanair calling itself Ryanair.'

. . .

'Through all these court cases, Lufthansa has probably created more publicity for us than we've had on any other route we've launched. We are now one of the best known brands in Germany thanks to Lufthansa suing us in every court in Germany.'

. . .

'Some of Europe's flag carriers are still grossly overstaffed, they run at losses, they sell below cost and they're incredibly inefficient. They are nancy boys. They're all screwed. Doomed.'

. . .

'The best reason to get out of bed is to beat the pulp out of your competition and they want to beat the pulp out of us.'

. . .

'There is a lot of stupid competition out there losing money. We are not reducing our low fares because we are a charity. There is some below-cost selling, everyone is at it. It's part of a land grab going on in Europe and we will always be lower than anyone else.'

. . .

'Code-sharing, alliances and connections are all about "How do we screw the poor customer for more money?"'

. . .

'If you put two expensive, loss making airlines together, then you just get another even more expensive and even greater loss making airline.'

. . .

'There are the three high-fares rapists - British Airways, Lufthansa and Air France.'

. . .

On being delayed at a Paris airport on an Air France flight: 'I was about to give them the "Do you know who I am?" thing, but thought that would have had me bumped out of the airport, never mind the flight. Fortunately there was a second flight, or I'd have had to beg to get on an easyJet flight.'

. . .

'Alitalia? I would not want it if it were given to me as a present.'

. . .

PLANE SPEAKING

To the boss of regional airline Aer Arann: 'Fuck off back to Connemara where you come from.'

. . .

On competing with Richard Branson's Virgin Express: 'I thought, OK Dickie, let's have you.'

. . .

'Branson got burned in the low-fares industry. Virgin Express was a dog. But he's done clearly very well with his other businesses; he's a multibillionaire. Branson is a genius for getting half a billion quid out of the Singaporeans for 49 per cent of his business.'

. . .

On the planned launch of Now Airlines, a Luton based competing low fares airline: 'Never.'

. . .

On the prospect of a merger with another airline: 'No thanks, I'd rather have a social disease.'

. . .

On offering advice to other airlines' bosses: 'They can fuck off and do their own work.'

. . .

IRELAND

'The airline industry is full of bullshitters, liars and drunks and we excel at all three in Ireland.'

. . .

'They don't call us the fighting Irish for nothing. We have been the travel innovators of Europe. We built the roads and laid the rails. Now it's the airlines. We will be the world's biggest airline.'

. . .

'I'm Irish and we don't have to prove anything. We bow to nobody. We are God's own children.'

. . .

'There is no shortage of ambition here. We'll stuff every one of them in Europe, we won't be second or third and saying, "Didn't we do well?" Ryanair shows what Irish people can achieve when we put our minds to it. We don't limit ourselves to being just good in Ireland.'

. . .

'We created the Irish tourism boom. The dogs in the street know what our contribution to tourism is. People do this bullshit analysis: why has Dublin boomed? Was it Temple Bar, U2 or the sunny Irish personality? Bullshit, we made Dublin cheap.'

. . .

'Did the tourists all start coming here in the mid-1980s because we had Guinness, nice personalities, were grand crack and it was a grand place for a stag party and all the rest of it? This place was like Albania in 1985.'

. . .

'I have a pain in my ear going around to all these airports saying we will fly to them from London, Frankfurt, Milan. They say: "We would really love, Monsieur, a route to Dublin or Shannon". We must reply: "Sorry, the Irish Government won't allow us". They are mystified until we explain that the Irish Government, through its airports, wants to screw us for every passenger we bring here.'

. . .

'Concerning the threat of moving the Ryanair headquarters from Dublin: there is no possibility of that whatsoever. I should say, however, that the Ryanair headquarters are not in Dublin, they are in Mullingar, which is obviously the centre of the universe.'

. . .

'We don't look upon ourselves as an Irish airline any more. We look upon ourselves as a European airline. Ryanair is effectively based in the UK.'

. . .

'It would be inconceivable that anyone would treat Ryanair as not Irish, otherwise we'd be homeless, or stateless. We're an Irish-owned, -operated and headquartered airline.'

. . .

'If we were an American computer company, the Irish Government would build statues to honour us, name buildings after us and ask what they can do for us to attract us to Ireland. However, because we are Irish, the Irish Government does not seem to want to follow our plan.'

.   .   .

'I am entitled to get a lot of criticism, I am opinionated, I am certainly not shy about holding forth on my opinions but regardless of whether I am being criticised, people in Ryanair are doing such an outstanding job. They get far too little credit in Ireland for what is by far and away and if not the most successful Irish business in the last twenty years.'

.   .   .

'Maybe it's just an Irish thing. We have spent our life having the shit kicked out of us. I'm a small Paddy over here in Europe trying to punch above his weight in terms of making noise. As Richard Branson demonstrated, the way to punch above your weight is to shout your mouth off.'

.   .   .

'This is one of the few islands in Europe and we do not have the option of cycling to the Continent.'

.   .   .

'Hey, they don't like us in Ireland, I don't care. We're not running for elections.'

.   .   .

'The country is bust and the European Central Bank is all that stands between us and a return to the poorhouse.'

'BRITAIN'S AWFUL AIRPORTS'

'The British Airport Authority are on a cocaine-induced spending spree. They are an overcharging, gold-plating monopoly which should be broken up.'

. . .

'The BAA want to spend £4 billion on an airport which should cost £100 million. £3.9 billion is for tree planting, new roadways and Norman Foster's Noddy railway so they can mortgage away the future of low-cost airlines. This plan is for the birds. BAA are a glorified shopping mall.'

. . .

'BAA are the worst airport builders in the western world. BAA stands for Britain's Awful Airports.'

. . .

On building new runways at Stansted: 'I think it's about bloody time. The British need to get their act together to compete with the French and the Germans. You have to develop more runways and terminals. There's been a lot of sitting on hands over here. Far too much time and attention is paid here to environmental groups and every other not-in-my-backyard you can think of.'

. . .

'If you live around Heathrow and you don't like living beside an airport, sell the house and move.'

. . .

'People can drive up the M11, they will walk barefoot over the fields for a cheap fare. What they are not going to do is pay 15 years in advance for some bloody marble Taj Mahal.'

. . .

'I could check in people in the car park, which would be cheaper than BAA. If they don't let me use their car parks we might let them check in at the truckers' car park on the M11.'

. . .

'A break-up of BAA would be the greatest thing that has happened to British aviation since the founding of Ryanair. Then airline customers would not be forced to endure the black hole of Calcutta that is Heathrow, or the unnecessary, overpriced palace being planned at Stansted.'

. . .

'Heathrow is a nightmare. You spend ages in queues and security checks when you could travel to Stansted with a fast train into the centre of London more cheaply and with less hassle. If you want to spend hundreds more pounds to not have to take a half-hour train journey then go ahead.'

. . .

PLANE SPEAKING

On the BAA being bought by a Spanish company:
'They're a Johnny Foreigner. It doesn't matter whether it is a British highwayman, a Spanish highwayman or an American highwayman. You are still getting robbed and that won't change until you break BAA's monopoly up.'

. . .

'Britain's air traffic control system have pissed away millions, millions of our money - it was 15 years late and it doesn't work. Stop building bloody marble palaces in Portsmouth and Brussels, and give us the service we need. ATC is a shambles. These guys can't recruit enough people, can't train them and can't run their own systems yet now they're looking for more money.'

. . .

'We're not going to pull out of Stansted, but we're not going to be robbed there either. It's Taj Mahals, gherkins and building projects for wannabe candidates for the House of Lords.'

. . .

'BAA would have you believe that people want to spend half their holiday at their wonderful airport buildings, spending money at their wonderful duty-frees. People actually want to spend 20 minutes at an airport? Park. Go through. Get on the plane. Get the hell out of the place.'

. . .

On asking Stansted Airport to waive landing charges:
'What we got back from the BAA was a polite two-word letter. The second word was "off". My pet pony would do a better job.'

AIRPORTS

On how to settle differences with Dublin Airport: 'With Semtex, preferably during a board meeting.'

. . .

'Dublin Airport spent £50 million on a five-storey extension which nobody wants to use. The new baggage hall is something designed by Russian architects. Pier C was designed by Aer Rianta to win an architectural competition rather than serve the needs of airlines.'

. . .

'The fact that Royal Jordanian will now be stopping off with 100,000 people for wee-wees in Shannon Airport will really guarantee the future of the airport and tourism in the mid-western region. Who knows, it might even create one or two jobs for lavatory cleaners in the area.'

. . .

'We simply allocate the new aircraft arrivals to airports all over Europe where, quite remarkably, airports, ministers and governments desperately vie with each other to offer us better deals.'

. . .

'Airports are coming to us saying, "Please open a base." Whichever airport provides us with the best package is the next new route we open.'

. . .

'We are a monopolist because we are able to dictate terms to airports.'

. . .

'We are going all over Europe where airports are falling over themselves to give us 25-year deals. They love us in England and we're treated like gods in Europe.'

. . .

'Bus operators carrying American tourists park near the tourist shops around Nassau Street in Dublin. Many of those shops give the bus drivers a kickback on the spend. I always wonder why airports do not do that. We are the bus drivers who deliver hundreds of thousands of passengers.'

. . .

'It is an open fact that some airports pay us to fly there.'

. . .

'We are not flying to airports that increase charges. Why do we do this? We are trying to lower costs for consumers. We want to reduce the cost of air travel. We are not bloody geniuses.'

. . .

'Lying governments have got together with airports to rip us off. We should say, "We aren't fucking taking it any more".'

. . .

On the Scottish Highlands and Islands airport authority: 'It's like the 1950s, you can't scratch your backside unless you get a subsidy first. It operates its airports like a tourist attraction.'

. . .

'There's all kinds of places in Scandinavia and down through Germany where NATO had bases during the Cold War. Even in the UK there's dozens of airports. When you look at an ordinary map you think there's no more airports – in actual fact the place is absolutely awash with airports. We look for the signs which show there's an airport somewhere and we go and talk with them.'

. . .

'Passengers will find their way to the airport if the air fares are low enough. Lufthansa spent the last two years swearing that Ryanair would not work in Germany and that Frankfurt-Hahn Airport would not work because the passengers would not go there. Two years later, passengers get there because they are saving €400 over the average fare charged by Lufthansa.'

. . .

On concerns from German airports operator Fraport that passengers would not fly from Hahn: 'That's bullshit. People will go there just because air fares are cheap. Frankfurt Hahn are charging us a very low cost per passenger. I would not tell my mother how much.'

. . .

'Sometimes there is not even a road to the airports we fly to. It is immaterial.'

DESTINATIONS

'Who wants to go to Gdansk? There ain't a lot there after you've seen the shipyard wall.'

. . .

'We've never done market research on any of our new routes. There are a lot of people, particularly in London, who are always looking for somewhere different. If you can fly to somewhere in Europe for £10 then you are going to fill 200 seats a day to almost anywhere.'

. . .

'If you can fly to the same destination with two airlines and one offers a fare which is a great deal less, then obviously you will choose the cheaper fare. There's no research needed for that.'

. . .

'People have laughed at some of our more unusual destinations, but we've never stopped flying to any of them due to lack of interest.'

. . .

'It's not as if JFK Airport is in Central Park or Heathrow is in Pall Mall. I don't give a toss where people want to go. I'm in the business of creating a market for people to go where they never have heard of. What we do is stimulate huge demand, and then capture it.'

. . .

'We had a presentation from a European government two weeks ago. The tourism and transport ministers came over and offered us a 20-year deal, with employment grants and our own terminal and everything. I had to go and meet them, though, you have to kiss someone's ass.'

. . .

'Cork is Mickey Mouse stuff. Do we care about Cork? Frankly, no. Bristol is bigger than Cork, nearly everything is bigger than Cork. The reality for Cork Airport is they put up costs and they lost passengers, and that will cost them. Get them to explain how that makes fucking business sense.'

. . .

'We would like to do more and base more aircraft here in Belfast and are working with the City Airport to get the runway extended. Let's get the planning permission through and let's ignore the mewling and puking from local residents which is a load of nonsense.'

. . .

'Glasgow-Prestwick until the mid-1960s relied on the transatlantic stop-over traffic. It had about two and a half million passengers per year. Prior to 1997 when we started to fly there, it had no passengers. The airport had been closed and there were sheep on the runway.'

. . .

'Liverpool is the low-fares regional airport for the north west of England. Liverpool doesn't have all the glass, bells and whistles that Manchester has, but passengers don't want glass, bells and whistles. It's always good to see Liverpool give Manchester a good kicking.'

. . .

'Newquay is the surf and dope capital of Britain. There's next to frig-all way of getting to Cornwall unless you fly. It's a fucking impossible nine-day hike. Closing that airport would be a disaster for surfer dudes, but also to loads of wealthy types who use us to commute up and down. I tell you, we'll have a bloody dogfight with the RAF. Watch out for those 737s on your wing, flyboys.'

. . .

'I was told to go to Malta because there is all-year-round sunshine, and the moment I step off the plane it starts raining. That's it, I'm pulling my airline out of Malta.'

. . .

'Our best-selling route at Luton is Esbjerg. On these flights, Danish passengers are coming over to watch football - the likes of Arsenal and Chelsea. Not Luton Town, they're a shit team.'

. . .

PLANE SPEAKING

'Twelve months ago I believed it made no sense flying to Poland. I've changed my mind. We will have one million passengers on our routes to Poland. We're happy to let our higher cost rivals get in there. We will follow when the time is right. We'll then push the others out to Russia, then Siberia.'

. . .

On opening new routes: 'We never want to be the explorers. They always get their heads shot off.'

. . .

'People won't pay four times more for flights that are four times longer, so fuck that.'

PUBLICITY

'All we do is go around, create a bit of controversy, do silly things, get our photograph taken in silly places and reduce the advertising money, and like that we can afford to keep the prices down.'

.   .   .

'You've got to keep people interested. We specialize in cheap publicity stunts.'

.   .   .

'If you make a lot of noise and fight with a lot of people you generate a lot of cheap publicity.'

.   .   .

'We prefer to dole out bon mots at regular weekly intervals.'

.   .   .

'Usually someone gets offended by our ads, which is fantastic. You get a whole lot more bang for your buck if somebody is upset.'

.   .   .

'Bookings peak for big advertisements. And they'll peak even more if somebody reacts badly to the advertisement.'

.   .   .

PLANE SPEAKING

On dressing up as St Patrick in London: 'Step this way, my children. I'm hoping to wind things up as quick as possible so I can have a few beers back in Dublin.'

. . .

On dressing up as Caesar in Rome: 'They're not used to someone going down and making a complete tit of himself.'

. . .

On dressing up as the Pope: '*Habemus* lowest fares, my children.'

. . .

'I don't mind dressing up in something stupid or pulling gormless faces if it helps. Frankly, I don't give a rat's arse about my personal dignity.'

. . .

'You cannot on the one hand court publicity as I do for Ryanair and then on the other hand say "Oh, I want to be alone. But it's a small price to pay".'

. . .

'If you live by the sword, you have to accept the occasional slash yourself.'

. . .

'I'm not doing something new as Richard Branson did it for years. We're doing what Branson did 20 years ago. You can make a lot of PR bang for your buck by being a little bit wacky.'

. . .

'Richard Branson will bore you to tears at a press conference. For all the PR, he is not the most entertaining man in the world. Apart from doing a photo-op with girls with big boobs, he is not that exciting. I try desperately not to get into the Branson stuff. This is not O'Leary Air.'

. . .

On consumer magazine *Which*?: 'I think you'd find more relevant consumer information in the *Beano* or the *Dandy* than in this magazine.'

. . .

On adding bigger breasts to the lady on the aircraft tail: 'She looked like a bloke with wings. Somebody said we should give her bigger boobs. So we did. Some quango said we were demeaning women. Fuck off. She's got bigger boobs. And the story got two half-pages in the *Sun*, worth £25,000 each.'

. . .

'Everyone here is delighted that our employee Brian Dowling made it into the Channel 4 *Big Brother* house. He's been two years in the Ryanair madhouse, which is perfect training. We will be holding his job for him and hope that he will be returning to us – unless, of course, he becomes an international superstar through this.'

. . .

When Dowling won *Big Brother*: 'I don't imagine he will want to come back if he is making a fortune. If he does, then we would be glad to have him, and perhaps we would use him in promotions. But if he is looking for appearance money he can feck off.'

. . .

After paying an £18,000 fine to the Advertising Standards Authority: 'All advertising is now vetted by three different people in the company, not only because we do not want to mislead consumers, but because we do not want to waste £18,000.'

. . .

'We got into horse racing because there are strong Irish links with Cheltenham. There is an annual exodus of drunken Paddies coming for four days of gambling and other recreation.'

. . .

To the editor of the City Diary at the *Guardian*: 'I realise that figures, accuracy and your good self have long been strangers. Everything in yesterday's Diary item about Ryanair was wrong.'

. . .

On being interviewed over lunch in his office by a *Financial Times* journalist: 'I forgot to charge you for the coffee, so you owe me one.'

. . .

On a Channel 4 *Dispatches* programme: 'Channel 4 can shove this programme up its jacksie.'

. . .

On a BBC TV *Panorama* programme about Ryanair: 'We got 30 minutes straight after *EastEnders*. You just can't buy that sort of publicity.'

. . .

With Ryanair's marketing manager, Sinead Finn, addressing an all-male press conference when she said: "I've got nine men in front of me. I don't know where to start": 'They're hardly all men. One of them is from the *Guardian*.'

. . .

At a press conference in Germany about a possible new transatlantic airline: 'In economy it will be very cheap fares, say about €10. And in business class it will be beds and blow jobs. In business class, it will all be free – including the blow jobs. What's the German for blow job? There is no German for blow job? Terrible sex life in Germany.'

. . .

'As long as it's not safety-related, there's no such thing as bad publicity.'

. . .

At a press conference, about a female reporter who crawled towards him to retrieve her microphone: 'If you want to stay on your knees, by all means, I'd encourage you. Sorry, I've forgotten the question – there was a very pretty girl on her knees there in front of me.'

. . .

'Welcome to the Ryanair press conference, where you can identify the person who is lying because his lips are moving. Everyone at a press conference is telling lies. I thought that was the first rule of journalism school. I thought we'd have the whole day to ourselves. And then fucking M&S goes and sacks someone. It's only women's knickers. Relax.'

. . .

At an over-hyped press conference: 'I'm a bit disturbed – the rumour went round we would announce my resignation and the share price rose three per cent.'

. . .

Halfway through a first-quarter results media presentation, aged 41, when his mobile phone rang: 'It was my mother. She wanted to know where I was.'

. . .

'I think we did make a mistake with the Sarkozy advertisement, but only because it wasn't particularly funny. I'm available to kiss and make up with Mrs Sarkozy any time she wants.'

. . .

'What are you going to ask me about next? Sex? Religion?'

LOVE

'I used to work seven days a week and usually 16-hour days. I had no time for girlfriends. I didn't have girlfriends for 10 or 15 years. I generally get on very well with women.'

. . .

'I'd love to spend the rest of my life on a beach in Barbados with a load of babes, but I'm striking out badly on that front.'

. . .

On being photographed with two models: 'It was a chance for me to dress up with a couple of pretty girls. It's a shitty job but someone has to do it.'

. . .

Before being married: 'I breed horses and cattle. It's the closest thing I have to a sex life. I spare no expense on the bulls, but now if only I could find a woman.'

. . .

'I have this theory that childbirth is so frightening, and you're so involved in it, that it's probably not very positive. But delivering a calf, well, that's fucking amazing.'

. . .

PLANE SPEAKING

On cancelling his first wedding: 'I'm not gay, before you ask. I crashed and burnt. I came very close to finding the one but it didn't happen, so it's kick on and just go back to work. I am depressingly single and I am living in hope that a woman will find me sufficiently attractive to settle down.'

. . .

On meeting his future wife: 'It was at a wedding that I was brutally dragged to because it was one of the Ryan's. She was a bridesmaid and she took pity on me.'

. . .

On his wedding guests: 'Aunty-fucking-Mavis? Who the fuck is Aunty-fucking-Mavis? My bride-to-be keeps asking me which I would prefer about wedding things I don't really have an opinion about either way. That's what I try and say, but it always comes out sounding like I don't give a fuck.'

. . .

'The wedding reception is going to be cheap. The honeymoon is going to kill me. We are going to Ryanair destinations, so at least I can get back quickly.'

. . .

On his bride arriving 35 minutes late for their wedding: 'She's coming here with Aer Lingus.'

. . .

'I never thought about selling my wedding to *Hello*! That's for the ones who can't afford to pay for their own weddings.'

. . .

'We threw out the last guest at 6.30 in the morning. We'd laid on low fare buses to get them home. I guarantee I won't be selling shares this year. The wedding got paid for so I'm all right.'

. . .

On whether marriage would make him more mellow: 'I don't think so. I hope not.'

. . .

'My experience of five weeks of fatherhood is that I want to spend more time at the office. I am staying in the guest room and I don't plan to re-emerge until my son is at least two years old and ready to take instructions. I'm taking the company approach to it: I am subcontracting everything.'

. . .

'I changed the first nappy in the hospital and, called upon in emergency, I will do another. I'm not one of these people who will be there doing the full-time father lark.'

. . .

'We have paternity leave but it's a bloody joke. It is bullshit legislation. You need a couple of days off because you've had a baby, but this nonsensical rubbish that you're entitled to days off parental leave for the first six years of a baby's life. Go and get a bloody job - get a life.'

. . .

'Since I got married I usually take one holiday during the year but if I can avoid it I will. I go to the Algarve with the family for two weeks, because I have to. And I can build the sandcastles with the children. You know, the sandcastle's fine for the first five minutes, and after that it's, "Oh Jesus, will someone come and rescue me!" I'm praying for a crisis.'

. . .

On his close friends: 'My wife, occasionally. My children on a good day.'

. . .

'I'm a fat cat when I fly in business class on long-haul flights. Otherwise I am not a fat cat. I am actually quite a slim cat. But my wife disagrees with that.'

. . .

Using the F-word 14 times at a press conference: 'I am in the first year of marriage. We've had our first row. She wanted to know where I was going to be in a week's time. How do I know that?'

. . .

On addressing students at Trinity College, Dublin: 'I'm not visiting because of some undying loyalty to Trinity. I'm here because of the high percentage of hot undergraduate tottie in the room.'

. . .

On introducing a management pay freeze: 'Someone's just frozen my effing pay. I'm trying to keep it quiet. I might have to tell my wife that we've got to cut back, that she'll have to start shopping at Lidl or Aldi rather than Tesco. The major sufferer here will be Mrs Willie Walsh. Mrs O'Leary may suffer as a consequence but she'll just have to tighten her belt for a year or two.'

. . .

On a business poll where women rated him less than men did: 'I have spent my whole life trying to increase my ratings with the ladies. Sadly, this survey confirms that it was all a waste of time.'

. . .

On radio when selecting his favourite pieces of music: 'I would have given you three pieces by U2, but that would have been fairly boring. If you are in your mid-40s in Ireland and you are not a life-long U2 fan then you should be shot. They are one of the great adverts for modern Ireland. They are one of the greatest things Ireland has produced in the last thirty years, apart from Ryanair.'

. . .

'Kenneth Williams had it right. Infamy, infamy, they fucking have it in for me.'

. . .

PLANE SPEAKING

On his business motto: 'It's economics. It's not society. I don't do bonding.'

. . .

'I will trip up at some stage. I'm not God, I might like to think I'm God, but I'm not.'

. . .

'I am very humble, shy and retiring. It is my humility that makes me the success I am today and also the fact that I am caring helps too.'

. . .

'I'm a genius, but I'm just too humble to say so.'

. . .

'I'm certainly er... memorable; some people think I am arrogant and a loud mouth, which in some cases would be hard to argue against, and - er - foul-mouthed. I don't wear a suit, which is not some Bransonesque thing that I never wear a suit, I just don't like coming to work in a suit.'

. . .

'I frankly don't care what people say about me or write about me. I didn't get into this job for the popularity. I'm only concerned about what the people in this airline think about me.'

HOME

'I grew up on a farm, and I'd always known that if I ever got any money I wanted to have my own house, my own farm. Then I got lucky and got more money and I wanted a grander house.'

. . .

'People go on about this magnificent mansion. It's a very nice family home. It's not one of those big palatial mansions, nor was it built to be. It was built as a weekend home for someone, but on a grand scale. I wouldn't want my kids rattling around in a ginormous fucking mansion.'

. . .

'My house isn't small but it feels fairly compact. If you have kids and the kids are growing up and bringing friends back, you don't want them to think they are arriving in Buckingham Palace.'

. . .

'I work my ass off six days a week, 12-hour days. I commute one hour to get here. I haven't got some bucolic lifestyle. Having grown up on a farm I would like my family to grow up on a farm. Like most people today I need to work harder and harder to make wealth for my family.'

. . .

'The facilities for bringing up kids in Mullingar are fantastic, and apart from the drug problem - which is everywhere – it's a great place to bring up kids.'

. . .

'I live in great fear of spending my eighty years and not making a difference. Even if you only pissed people off at least you made a difference.'

. . .

'I'm an Irish peasant at heart. I grew up on a farm in the Irish countryside, and now I live on a farm in the Irish countryside. You would impress fucking nobody if you drove to the paper shop on a Sunday morning in your Ferrari. They'd think you were a gobshite. And you probably would be. A big tractor, now, they might be impressed. But it doesn't get to the shop fast enough for me.'

. . .

'Would I see myself driving a tractor five days a week? No.'

'The word "buggers" is a term of endearment in Mullingar.'

. . .

'My hobby is agriculture. That's perhaps what I will do for a few years.'

. . .

'I didn't want to be in Charolais bulls because Tony Ryan and Tony O'Reilly and all those guys were into Charolais. I didn't want to be pricking around as the latest idiot with his Charolais cows.'

. . .

'I wanted something which was a native breed to Ireland, which means Whitehorns or Angus. The Angus were easy calving, they are very easy to handle. For someone who farms two days a week they were perfect. I spent one week on a course about Low-Cost Artificial Insemination Techniques for Angus Heifers. Frankly, it was a load of bull.'

. . .

On a prize bull: 'All he does is makes babies and eat. That's what I look forward to doing when I retire.'

. . .

On buying a €42,000 prize bull: 'As you know I have a long-standing policy of not commenting on rumour or speculation, regardless of how much bullshit is involved.'

. . .

'I'm always polite.'

. . .

PLANE SPEAKING

'Privately and personally, I don't think I'm quite as obnoxious as I come across.'

. . .

'They love me in Spain, Portugal and Italy, but that may be because they haven't got to know me.'

. . .

'I never comment on anything to do with my private life. And that's private, sorry. Look, I'll answer any question on Ryanair, but when it comes to myself the answer is, "There is no answer".'

SPORT

'I fell off a horse at the age of four and I realised it was a stupid activity. My brothers and sisters didn't realise how stupid it was and kept going.'

. . .

On owning racehorses: 'It's 90 per cent frustration and 10 per cent fun. But the 10 per cent fun vastly outweighs the other side. The owner is the mug at the bottom of the food chain. As long as you know that, you'll be OK. But you have to know you will lose your money. Which makes me an idiot.'

. . .

'I keep a couple of race horses, but that's kind of chump change. I don't know enough about them to be able to train them or ride them or anything like that.'

. . .

'As a businessman, I can make plans and I can have influence, but in jump racing I have to accept that the trainer and the jockeys make all the important decisions. I just pay the bills.'

. . .

'But if you like the people in jump racing, as I do, then the sport becomes a great social activity. It's a perfect pursuit for stupid rich guys.'

. . .

'I have been able to indulge my passion for horse racing. Unfortunately, unlike the airline, they don't tend to go anywhere very fast.'

. . .

'In five years we expect to be carrying 100 million passengers, which we hope will keep our share price flying and keep me in racehorses, which is the only reason I go to work anyway.'

. . .

'The Cheltenham Festival is a great Irish institution - for me, the Olympics of racing – although still an occasion to be routinely beaten up by the English.'

. . .

'I came to Cheltenham on Ryanair with 188 other Irish passengers. The plane was full.'

. . .

When his horse War of Attrition won the Cheltenham Gold Cup: 'Unbelievable, I've died and gone to heaven. Free flights for everyone this evening. I'll pay for them all myself. Tonight we shall have a couple of very quiet drinks soberly before catching the 9pm Ryanair to Twickenham to watch Ireland beat England. On time, too. And we'll be paying for our luggage.'

. . .

'I remember as a kid bunking off from school to put money on the Grand National. I'd say the biggest bet I've had was fifty quid. The bet was each way. It's the accountant in me. You can take the man out of accountancy but you can't take the accountant out of the man.'

. . .

When his horse Hear The Echo won the Irish Grand National: 'People asked me earlier should they back him. I told them no way. I thought he was going out for a run to keep himself warm.'

. . .

On visiting the gym: 'I like to look up and down a slim girl's rear. Sadly there's not that many of them. They're a bunch of old sweaty farts.'

. . .

'When I was younger I dreamed of playing football for Manchester City. I've followed Manchester City closely since 1967 - I was six and it was the last time they won the league. It's an experience rather like jump racing, really, in that the good days are far outnumbered by the bad and you have to learn to take your beatings.'

. . .

PLANE SPEAKING

'I got a letter last year from someone who said that they had 30 per cent of Manchester City, wanting to know would I be interested in buying their share. They had heard I was a fan. I wrote back a very nice letter saying "Thank you very much, I've been a lifelong supporter of Man City. They've broken my heart on numerous occasions but I'll confine my support to going to Maine Road about twice a year".'

. . .

'Can you imagine buying a controlling interest in an English soccer team? You'd be all over the back pages of the papers. That is not what running Ryanair is about. You'd be giving interviews about dealing with players' agents. It's completely insane. I confine my insanities to horse racing, which at least is relatively cheap, cheap in the context of football teams.'

. . .

'Have you noticed that one way you can win the World Cup is to have a right-wing dictatorship?'

. . .

'As for England's chances in the World Cup, I'm not sure - I think when push comes to shove, you simply have a spineless team.'

. . .

'We're Irish - we're used to losses. England come over and kick the shit out of us nine years out of 10. An age-old Irish custom to give an English guy a kick when he's on the ground.'

WEALTH

'I was always driven and I was always competitive. Maybe I was kicked by somebody at some stage, but if I was I don't remember it. Why are you the way you are? I haven't a bloody bull's notion. Would I want to spend a lot of time analysing myself? No.'

. . .

'The harder you work the luckier you get. You make your own breaks.'

. . .

'I come to work because it's fun. It's far better than poncing around on a beach somewhere.'

. . .

'I'm not into art, never have been. I've nothing on the left side of the brain, or whatever side of the brain artistic stuff is on.'

. . .

'I thought the first £1 million was going to be like multiple orgasms, greatest night of your life. But nothing. So you think, "I've got to double this and make two." Then four, then eight. At a certain point, don't ask when it is, money stops being important.'

. . .

PLANE SPEAKING

'If you take it all away tomorrow, I will be really pissed off. Racehorses and cattle are my poison, but I don't live a high life.'

. . .

'I buy everything low-cost. I buy cheap shirts. I buy cheap jeans. I buy cheap shoes. It's a philosophy. I'm just cheap.'

. . .

'I'm in the tragic position of selling 10 per cent of my holding in Ryanair a year and still having 90 per cent of my wealth tied up in this airline. I'm selling shares for good, boring portfolio-management reasons. It doesn't make sense to have everything tied up in one asset.'

. . .

'I thought it was time to get the hell out before the stock market crashed. Then the market upturned, which just goes to show what a moron I am. I stuck it in the post office. The money is spread around banks and post offices. I'm using it to staunch my farming losses.'

. . .

'Some people may be unhappy with the share sales. That's fine. Some people think the management should be locked in indentured fucking slavery for ever.'

. . .

'I don't want to be like the dot com fucking goons. My policy is that I'm going to take a lump off the table every year. Dotcoms were the biggest demonstration of asinine stupidity. They were all running around being billionaires on paper and nobody took money off the table.'

. . .

'I want some certainty that I have some cash sitting in the post office if, God forbid, terrorists blow up the London airports or we make a complete dog's balls of this operation.'

. . .

'I might leave it all to someone in the pub so they could have the biggest party in the history of Christendom. At least they would get more out of it than I did.'

. . .

'I'm just a poor farmer from Westmeath. Well, maybe not that poor.'

. . .

'With the amount of tax that I've paid, Jesus, I've paid for my own airport by now. I paid over €20 million last year. But who wants to live in Monaco when you can live in Mullingar? It has so much more to offer. Although if you were being asked to pay 60 or 70 per cent in tax, I'd be gone in a flash.'

. . .

PLANE SPEAKING

On writing a tax cheque for €14 million: 'This is the most expensive stunt I've ever pulled. Paying my taxes is the price I pay for the privilege of living in the independent republic of Mullingar.'

. . .

On his dress sense: 'People think I do this because I'm some sort of a rebel, but it's not. It's just very easy to get up in the morning and find a blue shirt and a pair of jeans. You don't have to think.'

. . .

When being photographed wearing a suit: 'Don't make me look like a boring bastard in a suit.'

. . .

'I have a Mercedes 500. Not because I like the Mercedes 500, but because it's a big, comfortable fucking car.'

. . .

'Do we carry rich people on our flights? Yes, I flew on one this morning and I'm very rich.'

RETIREMENT

'I am just a big mouth on top of a fantastic group of people. I think it is shite to say that I am indispensable. The company stands on its own.'

. . .

'In many ways I have been one of their strengths, and one of their weaknesses. But when you are big, you have to know when the entrepreneurial gobshite has to go.'

. . .

'In the future the company will need a chief executive who is different than I am. As the biggest carrier in Europe, they would have no use for someone who runs around in jeans and calls politicians idiots and says that the EU Commission is made up of Communists.'

. . .

'I think you need me to hand over to somebody who talks about caring about the environment and old people and fucking jungles and fish in the sea and all that shite.'

. . .

'You need to step away before you believe you really can walk on bloody water.'

. . .

'If I was just to think, "I'm 43 and I'll be here for the next 20 years," I'd rather be shot now.'

. . .

'I won't be gone in three or five years time. But I have promised my wife that I will be.'

. . .

'I plan to go on and on and on, like Chairman Mao.'

. . .

'I'll never stop. Better to wear away than to rust away. I like work - it's like a holiday.'

. . .

'My plan has always been remarkably consistent. I intend to step down in the next two or three years. It's a bit of a moveable feast, but one day I'll be right.'

. . .

'My scenario here is that I'll be gone out of here in 12 months' time. That's been the plan every year since 1988, and it's the only thing that keeps me sane.'

. . .

'You have to remember that I said I would retire in 1992, that I would retire in 1995, and I think again in 1998. Some of my forecasts have not turned out to be terribly accurate.'

. . .

'I was ready to step down a year ago but now everyone says we're in the shit, so I'm staying.'

. . .

'They'll find somebody else equally humble, shy and retiring, but maybe not as good-looking.'

. . .

On starting a new long-haul low-cost transatlantic service: 'It's a small retirement project. I would invest in it, get it off the ground and make it fly. But I would have the wrong image for sexy business class. People would say O'Leary will charge you for reclining your seat. I don't think you can have me marketing it because I'm too attached – certainly in European minds – to being cheap and cheerful. But I'm thinking of calling the airline something sexy like O'Leary Air or Ego Air.'

. . .

'It would be very difficult for me to don a tie and go on to committees. Could you imagine me looking for a knighthood? Puke. The weakness of British Airways is that everyone is looking for a knighthood.'

. . .

'I'll be making the world a better place - by taking a vow of silence.'

. . .

PLANE SPEAKING

'I don't look back at all. I'm 47, and I'm not going to be sitting here pulling wool out of my navel wishing I had done something differently. This is the most fun you can have with your clothes on. There's a danger that I'll self combust.'

. . .

'I'm in blooming health. Only the good die young, so in that case, I'm going to live to a ripe old age.'

. . .

'I think there will be dancing in the street at the idea of O'Leary leaving Ryanair.'

. . .

'My eulogy will probably begin with, "He was a jumped-up little bollox" and hopefully will end with, "He lived fast and died young".'